GW01080907

There's nothing easy — . we love our kids and want them to be happy, safe, and successful in everything they do. Naturally, we worry—it simply comes with the territory. We worry about whether our kids are doing well in school, what kind of friends they're hanging around with, if they're drinking or using other drugs, and most of all, how to keep them safe from all the violence that exists.

Our protective instinct makes us wish we could keep our kids close at hand twenty-four hours a day, making sure they're doing the right thing and staying out of harm. But we can't. Even though we want desperately to keep our kids safe, we can't protect them when they're out of our sight—at school, with friends, or out on the streets. And even if we could, we know that we have to let our children grow up and gradually leave the nest.

> **How can we stop worrying and start trusting that our kids will make the right choices?**

So where does that leave us? How can we stop worrying and start trusting that our kids will make the right choices in an often dangerous world where violence, alcohol, and other drug use have become the norm? The answer is this: By **EMPOWERING** our kids. By helping them learn how to be sensible, safe, and secure.

That's what every parent wants. We want our children to develop into confident, competent individuals who are able to stand on their own, avoid peer pressure, and be accepted and respected wherever they go. We want them to grow up to be responsible family members and upstanding citizens. We want them to learn how to make healthy choices that ensure their wellbeing at every stage of their lives.

And we can. IF we're willing to start **EMPOWERING** them.

One of the surest ways to empower our kids is to teach them how to handle their anger in nonviolent ways.

When kids learn from their parents how to handle anger appropriately, they are empowered to act sensibly so they'll stay safe and feel more secure inside. Not all parents are good role models when it comes to handling their own anger appropriately. For many parents, trying to juggle the demands of family and work creates tremendous worry and frustration that comes out as anger—and it doesn't always come out in the right way. When anger *is* expressed *inappropriately*, it can be contagious. For example, when we lash out or yell at our partner or our kids, they feel angry too, and may take it out on someone else in the family who then takes *their* anger out on the next person who gets in the way. Even the family dog can be a victim of anger if he or she happens to be in the line of fire. This domino effect leaves *everyone* in the family feeling battered, bruised, and victimized.

Ideally the family setting is one place where kids should never have to worry about anger expressed inappropriately or in violent ways. To help our kids feel safe and secure, we'll want to explore how to deal with our own anger in a healthy way.

Why is learning to handle anger so important? Because when anger isn't expressed in an appropriate way, it becomes violence. We define violence as *any mean word, look, sign, or act that hurts another person's body, feelings, or possessions.* Violence is *not* what we want our kids to learn. For example, when we get angry, we may hurt our kids' feelings by using **words** as **weapons,** words that are sarcastic, accusing, or critical. Too often, kids today may go *beyond* using words as weapons. Instead, they use fists, knives, guns, or other weapons to deal with their anger. So it's urgent that we teach our kids—and ourselves—how to handle our anger *before* it handles us!

Parents don't intentionally express anger inappropriately. Some simply haven't learned how and so they end up using the same ineffective methods they observed as kids growing up in their own family. It's never too late to learn an effective and constructive way to express our anger. If we choose not to learn, we may inadvertently teach our kids to handle anger in violent ways such as:

Using words as weapons

Although most of us grew up with the saying, "Sticks and stones may break my bones, but words will never hurt me," in fact, words do hurt. Using sarcasm, put-downs, judgments, or name calling makes our kids feel threatened and insecure. The message is "*You're no good*" or "*You're* unlovable" rather than, "What I'm angry about is your *behavior*." Our kids learn to imitate us by being verbally disrespectful or abusive to others around them.

Using threats or intimidation

Threatening or intimidating kids is a form of violence. When we threaten or intimidate our kids, for instance, saying: "Do that again, and you'll really have something to worry about!" or "Just wait 'til your father comes home!" we frighten our kids, which makes them resentful instead of receptive. It causes them to lose respect and trust for us. Our kids may deal with their resulting feelings of fear and resentment by threatening or intimidating others to get even. Or they may turn to alcohol or other drugs to numb their feelings.

Using physical violence

There is never any excuse for using force to express violence toward kids. Expressing anger by hitting, kicking, or hurting kids in *any* way is entirely inappropriate and extremely destructive. Physical abuse teaches our kids to use violence to get even or get what they want, instead of expressing their feelings in a constructive and positive way.

It's clear that using words as weapons or physical force to handle anger is unacceptable and gives kids the wrong message. But there's another, less obvious way some parents have learned to handle anger and that is to deny the anger—to pretend they don't feel it—that everything is okay, when it isn't. But "stuffing" feelings doesn't work. When we deny our anger it bottles up inside and builds like hot air in a balloon. Ultimately, we too may either explode and lash out in violent ways or shut down and feel depressed. Like our children, that is when we are most vulnerable to using alcohol or other drugs to handle our anger.

Even though our kids *act* as though they are ignoring us, they constantly watch what we do. Consequently, they learn to *act* as we do. For example, let's say we're angry that our husband (or wife) is an hour late coming home from work. The lovely dinner we've labored over is now cold, everyone in the family is hungry, and by the time our spouse sits down at the table we've reached the boiling point. When he or she comments on the lukewarm casserole, we explode, screaming, "If you say one word about my meatloaf, I'll dump it on your head!"

There are other, much more effective ways to handle anger without shouting, name-calling, hitting, kicking, threatening, or using a weapon to get even. And here's the good news: Learning to handle anger can be easy! All we need to do is learn how to use these four **ABCD** steps. Here's what each stands for:

A is for AWARE

When we *know* we're getting angry (our face turns red, we feel hot inside, our fists are clenched, we start to shout), we can move on to Step B.

B is for BACK OFF

When we give ourselves time to cool down and sort out what's wrong and what we're really feeling, we can move on to Step C.

C is for CHOICES and CONSEQUENCES

Now we can consider the choices we have for handling our anger and the consequences that could result from each choice, which leads us to Step D.

D is for DECIDE and DO

Having considered our choices and the consequences that are likely to happen with each choice, we can decide which one is safest for everyone and do it!

The ABCD steps empower kids to *choose* how to handle their anger in *every* situation and to be responsible for their choices. Kids learn an extremely important lesson: that no one can *make* them express anger in violent ways. It's *their* choice.

The next six scenarios illustrate how to successfully use the **ABCD** steps to teach our kids how to deal with anger without violence:

SCENARIO ONE: Becky runs into the kitchen where Mom is, crying and screaming, "Michael hit me!" Michael runs in after her, Becky turns and swings at him. "Stop that," says Mom, asking, "What's going on here?" Michael angrily defends himself, complaining that his little sister keeps taking his things without asking. "Is that right?" Mom asks Becky. "I was *going* to put it back," she replies. Mom tells Becky that it's not okay to take Michael's toys without asking. Then she turns to Michael and says, "I understand why you're mad, but it's never okay to hit anyone, no matter how angry you are." Both Michael and Becky lose a privilege for acting inappropriately. "That's not fair!" complains Michael. "She made me hit her!" Becky retaliates with, "Did not!" Mom puts a hand on each of her children's shoulders and acknowledges that it's okay for each of them to *feel* angry but that she expects them to learn how to handle their anger in the *right* way.

Mom is on the right track. She introduces the **ABCD** steps by engaging her kids in the following dialogue. First, she explains Step **A**—being *aware*—by asking Michael to describe what it feels like inside when he's angry. Michael answers, "I feel hot, like I'm going to explode." Mom says, "Good," then suggests that when he feels that way, he take the next step, **B**—*back off and cool down*. She then turns to Becky and asks what she thinks it means to "back off." Her young daughter shows that she understands this concept by saying, "Like stop? Or go somewhere 'til you're not so mad?" "Yes, good!" says Mom, reinforcing the idea that taking a time off to cool down helps us to think about what's happened and how we might *really* feel inside.

Because anger is often a cover for *other* underlying feelings, Mom gives some examples, such as feeling hurt or sad. Mom goes on to show how being *aware* of your feelings and *backing off* allows us to proceed to Step **C**—thinking what choices we have for handling our angry feelings and what the consequences could be. She reminds her kids that hitting, calling names or breaking someone's possessions to get even is one choice, but it's the *wrong* choice. Michael defends hitting Becky by saying, "But I *told* her to not touch my stuff but she doesn't listen!" Mom asks Michael to consider some other choices. He can't come up with any and complains that Mom won't *let* him lock his door, and if he *tells* her when Becky takes something, that's *snitching*. So what's he supposed to do? Mom responds by offering some other options: It's not snitching if Michael comes to her when Becky keeps taking his things without asking. "On the contrary," she explains, "that's a *sensible* choice because it prevents a fight and keeps everyone *safe*—a good example of Step **D**—*deciding* what's sensible and safe and *doing* it.

Scenario One illustrates the importance of making it clear to our kids that it's okay to *feel* angry, but it's *not* okay to *express* anger with violence. So what is an appropriate way for kids to express anger? One good way is for kids to talk their feelings out with someone—a parent, another adult, or a trusted friend. Our kids do need to be shown how to express anger appropriately by their parents, especially when their parents have had the experience of backing off and getting perspective, as we see in the next scenario.

SCENARIO TWO: Jenny is talking on the phone, carrying on about a classmate she's furious at, using every four-letter word in the book: "She's such a slut! Everyone says so. She's always throwing herself at boys. And she's a lying little bi...."

Jenny suddenly realizes her dad has overheard her and quickly gets off the phone. Dad calmly says, "Jenny, what did Mom and I tell you about calling people names?" Jenny self-righteously retorts, "Well, she's been spreading stuff about *me* all over school!" Dad says, "If that's true, you have a right to *feel* angry, but we expect you to learn to handle your anger in the right way," thus making a distinction between Jenny's right to *feel angry* and it not being okay to express her anger with name-calling or gossip.

Jenny thinks she *is handling* her anger by confiding in her friend Tracy. Dad sets her straight by explaining how gossiping and spreading rumors is really using words as weapons—and that's violence. He reminds her to use the **ABCD** steps. First, he acknowledges that she's already *aware* of her anger and suggests that now she needs to *back off* and think about what she's *really* feeling. "Can't I just be mad?" Jenny wonders. "Sometimes," Dad agrees, "but I think there's more to this." Dad's insight helps Jenny realize that she's actually *worried* that her friends might believe the lies and turn against her, so she'd better fight back. Dad offers Jenny a different choice: "Why not talk to your friends and tell them how you feel?" He reassures her that her real friends will understand and stick by her, which Jenny is willing to consider.

The scenario above reveals how the **ABCD** steps can uncover other feelings that anger sometimes masks, such as hurt, sadness, fear, or jealousy. When we teach our kids to identify the real feelings beneath their anger, they are more empowered to make non-violent choices in expressing their feelings. Being able to identify and name their feelings also helps kids to stop blaming others and to take responsibility for their own part in conflicts or misunderstandings, as we see in the next scenario.

SCENARIO THREE: Ron comes into the living room carrying his schoolbooks. Concerned, Mom asks why he's late, and Ron explains that he got detention for yelling at Ms. Moody, his algebra teacher. "What happened?" Mom asks. Ron can't wait to explain how justified he was in talking back to his teacher. "She's out to get me," he begins. "It's like, Brad was messing around behind her back, but she yelled at *me* instead. That really burned me but I *tried* not to let it get to me—*you* know—that **ABCD** stuff," Ron throws in to show Mom he's really tried to get with the program. "So I didn't say anything to her until after class," he continues, "but then she acted like she *knew* it was me, so I called her a jerk."

Ron feels justified that he's in the right. But Mom sees it differently. She explains to her son that when you try to tell someone you're angry or upset by blaming them or calling them names, it just makes things worse. Ron is told that he needs to apologize to Ms. Moody tomorrow for calling her a name, and that it would help to tell her how he *felt* about what happened by using an "I statement." For example, "I feel mad when you blame me for something I didn't do." Ron accepts Mom's advice, but says he still thinks his teacher is unfair. Mom says she understands, and tells Ron to let her know how it goes tomorrow at school.

Ron's Mom does an effective job of using the **ABCD** steps to help her son look at how he had handled the episode with his teacher. She affirms his feelings but also explains why choosing to call Ms. Moody a name wasn't appropriate and certainly hadn't worked to his advantage. She tells Ron to apologize and suggests he tell his teacher his true feelings in an appropriate way that will yield better results. Notice how she suggests that Ron use an "I statement" to express his anger to Ms. Moody, instead of a "You statement," which usually casts blame or accuses the person. "I statements," for example, "I feel angry," or "I feel hurt when you pick on me," simply describe how we feel. "*You* statements" though, for example, "You don't like me because you're always picking on me," or "You think you can boss me around," threaten others and can actually turn arguments or disagreements into violent

confrontations. Teaching kids how to use "I statements," also empowers them to use their power
appropriately to take care of themselves instead of
feeling victimized by other peoples' behavior, as is evi-
dent in the next scenario.

SCENARIO FOUR: Michael asks his dad for advice.
"I don't know what to do," he says. "This kid at
school is always trying to start a fight with me. He
calls me names and tries to push me around in front
of everyone. I've tried that **ABCD** stuff, but I can't
talk to him. Now, I *have* to fight him because if I
back down, I'll look like a wimp." Dad sympathizes
with Michael, who clearly doesn't want to fight, but
doesn't see any other choice under the circumstances.
Thankfully, Dad knows just what to say. "No one can
make you fight, he explains, adding, "If you let this
kid get to you, you give your power away. *You have
the power* to choose *not* to fight him." "But I'm so
mad I've *got* to do something," Michael says, to which
his Dad responds, "Let's go shoot some hoops and
talk about it some more."

Notice that Dad empowers Michael to walk away
from a fight and *doesn't* tell him to use his power to
fight back. In doing so, Dad has taken a potentially
violent situation and turned it around by using the
ABCD steps: He's encouraged Michael to be aware of
his anger. He's helped him back off and take an objec-
tive look at what he's really feeling—afraid of looking
like a wimp! He's offered Michael a new way to per-
ceive the situation and encouraged him to decide on a

safer, more empowering approach to handling his anger by walking away from a fight. And Dad has helped his son work off some steam with healthy exercise.

Ideally, parents would always prefer to have the wisdom, patience and fortitude to guide their kids in expressing their anger the right way. But sometimes we're so stressed out that *we* get hooked into fighting *with* our kids, as we see in the next scenario.

SCENARIO FIVE: Mom is really worried about how much time Jenny spends with her friend Sheila whom Mom disapproves of. On more than one occasion Sheila has skipped school, and she's constantly being grounded by her parents for staying out past curfew. After trying several times to tell Jenny how she feels, Mom finally puts her foot down, yelling, "I don't want you hanging around with that Sheila anymore! She's a little troublemaker and a bad influence!" Jenny lashes back, screaming, "You're *always* putting her down just because her parents are divorced. I hate you! I'm never going to talk to you again!"

We've all had angry scenes with our kids from time to time. As in any close relationship, we get angry at our kids and they get angry at us. So how are we supposed to teach our kids to handle their anger at *us* especially when we aren't expressing *our* anger in an appropriate way? Here's how Mom can rectify the situation:

Mom: "I know you're angry at me and that's okay. But there's a *right* way to tell me how you feel instead of threatening me. That makes it hard for me to listen to what you're saying."

Jenny: "Okay. I feel *really* mad at you when you trash my friends. It's not fair! You just don't like Sheila."

Mom: "I'm sorry I made judgments about Sheila. I worry that *you'll* get in trouble at school, too, if you hang around with her."

Jenny: "Okay, but just because *she* does some dumb things doesn't mean *I* will. I'm not a baby, you know."

Mom: "Yes, I know."

Mom and Jenny's second, more successful attempt to resolve their conflict teaches Jenny two important lessons: First, that it is possible to express parent/child anger in a constructive way. Second, how to use the same skills in other relationships outside of the family. But then there are those times when we, as parents, are so angry and frustrated that we simply lose it and try to force our kids to feel or act the way we want them to. What we need to learn to do, though, is express that anger and frustration appropriately. We have to take a deep breath and get hold of ourselves so that we can avoid expressing our anger in violent ways that we're bound to regret, as the final scenario illustrates.

SCENARIO SIX: Michael walks in the front door tracking globs of mud across the living room carpet. Dad's eyes bug out, his hair stands on end, he's ready to explode at his son. Terrified, Michael backs away, as Dad starts on a tirade, "Michael, I'm *so* angry with you! This is the third time I've told you not to track mud on the carpet." Realizing he's nearing the boiling point, Dad struggles to regain his composure, then calmly tells Michael, "I need to calm down for awhile. I expect you to clean this up *now* and we'll discuss the consequences after dinner." Michael, relieved to see his dad calming down, answers in a resigned voice, "Okay, Dad."

Notice how Dad used the **ABCD** steps in order to handle his *own* anger. The steps work for grownups, too! Dad kept a potentially explosive situation from happening by being *aware* that he was very angry, by *backing off* and calming down, by *choosing* to tell Michael what he expected him to do, and by *deciding* to table discussing the consequences until after dinner.

Teaching our kids how to use the **ABCD** steps to handle anger gives them a real sense of power, safety, and security. But if we want our kids to handle *their* anger, we have to remember to handle *ours*. In other words, we want to be congruent in our words and actions— saying what we mean, and meaning what we say. This means walking the way we talk, practicing what we preach, so our kids will take us seriously, respect us, and follow our example. If we use angry insults or put-downs, if we *tolerate* malicious gossip, bullying, or accept fighting as a way to solve problems, our kids get the message that we think it's sometimes okay to express anger with violence. We need to be consistent to be effective. When adults *tolerate* violent behavior by kids, the kids interpret the tolerance as *permission* to act that way. Then they feel *entitled* to use violence to express anger or settle disputes, which is exactly the message we don't want them to get.

If we want our kids to learn how to be peacemakers, regardless of what conflicts arise, we must take a firm stand: Violence is *not okay.* We *won't* tolerate it. There's no better way to keep our kids sensible, safe, and secure.